CW01310293

# BE FASCINATED!

*An answer
to the big questions*

Manel Salido

BE FASCINATED! An answer to the big questions
Original title in Spanish: ¡Fascinaos! Una respuesta a las grandes preguntas

English translation by Kristofer Montenegro
Copyright © Manel Salido 2024
Cover design: Henry Rodríguez
Layout: signocomunicacion.es

No part of this publication may be reproduced, stored in a retrieval system or transmitted in any form or by any means, without the prior permission in writing of the copyright holders, nor to be otherwise circulated in any form of binding or cover other than that in which it is published, within the limits established by law and under the legally provided warnings.

# INDEX

ACKNOWLEDGEMENTS ..................................................... 7
INTRODUCTION ................................................................. 9

**I. BE FASCINATED!** ........................................................ 11
1. Be fascinated! ................................................................ 13

**II. WHY ARE WE NOT FASCINATED?** ...................... 15
2. Why are we not fascinated? ........................................ 17
3. Free will and the self .................................................... 21
4. The fear of death .......................................................... 25
5. Spirituality ..................................................................... 35
6. Minimalism ................................................................... 37

**III. THE BIG QUESTIONS** ........................................... 43
7. Who are we? .................................................................. 45
8. Where did we come from? .......................................... 47
9. Where are we heading? ................................................ 49
10. What happens after death? ....................................... 51
11. What is the meaning of life? ..................................... 53
12. Freedom and free will ................................................ 57
13. Free will and the self—a settled question? ............. 61
14. The dilemma between determinism and free will ... 65
15. Voluntary and involuntary actions ........................... 67

## IV. WHAT CHANGES ONCE YOU KNOW THERE IS NO SELF OR FREE WILL? ....... 69

16. What do we do once we understand there is no self or free will? ....... 71
17. Hatred ....... 75
18. Why love but not hate ....... 79
19. Merit and praise ....... 81
20. Pride, arrogance and disdain ....... 83
21. Humility ....... 87
22. Self-esteem ....... 89
23. Shame ....... 93
24. Envy ....... 95
25. Duty ....... 97
26. Repentance and remorse ....... 99
27. Willpower ....... 101
28. Control ....... 105
29. Responsibility ....... 111
30. Guilt ....... 115
31. Justice ....... 119
32. Punishment and reward ....... 121
33. Revenge ....... 125
34. Forgiveness ....... 127
35. Personal relationships ....... 131

## V. CONCLUSIONS ....... 135
36. Conclusions ....... 137

WHERE TO FIND MORE INFORMATION ....... 141
QUOTES ABOUT FREE WILL ....... 145

# ACKNOWLEDGEMENTS

I have been very lucky to count on the selfless aid of Esteve Freixa i Baqué, Professor of Epistemology and Behavioral Sciences, PhD in Psychology and Licentiate in Philosophy and Letters. His proofreading of the book down to the smallest details has been of great value in addressing mistakes and adding concepts to correctly express the ideas from the point of view of the behavioral sciences. It is a pleasure to continue chatting with him from time to time, both because of the friendly conversation and because of how much you learn about human behavior and almost anything by talking with him.

Clemente García Novella, author of *¿Dónde está Dios, papa? Las respuestas de un padre ateo* (Where is God, Dad? The answers of an atheist father) and *Ser feliz es fácil* (Being Happy is Easy), has been by my side correcting every chapter as I was writing them. Having a friend like him along for the ride from the beginning has made me really enjoy writing and never feel lonely. His comments and corrections turned out to be a great lesson on how to expose ideas and how to use language, with nuances that I had never been able to appreciate. I have enjoyed it very much and learned a lot, both from his linguistic corrections and from his criticism of sometimes wrong or poorly expressed ideas.

Kristofer Montenegro has introduced me to the ideas of several of the scientists and philosophers whose works have inspired much of this book, that he has translated into English. Together we have matured these and other ideas in long conversations. We even enjoy discussing some disagreements without letting this affect our friendship at all, which is very enriching. During the writing of the book, he pointed out the arguments that needed correction or further elaboration.

Henry Rodriguez has helped me to better express some ideas and to realize several mistakes. He has been supporting me since I started a blog, which he suggested I write. He created and maintains the website **www.fascinaos.com** (be fascinated) and has designed the cover of this book.

Miquel Vanyó has collaborated with me for several years now, organizing conferences and other activities related to science and critical thinking. He has helped me to take a better approach on some ideas and has translated the book into Catalan.

Thanks to them all. And also to you, the person who is now starting to read this book.

# INTRODUCTION

When our ancestors asked questions about their existence and that of the world, they often made up magical powers, spirits and gods to explain what they could not understand. These kinds of beliefs have profoundly influenced the way we view life. In fact, much of humanity still believes in a god and an afterlife. And, although many of us no longer hold these beliefs, we often continue to think of ourselves as something akin to a soul: a self that has a body and directs many of its actions thanks to its free will.

Not believing in either a god or an afterlife is often seen as a cause of unhappiness. Simply talking about the nonexistence of free will and the self is perceived as a threat to our well-being. These fears are absolutely unfounded. Being aware of the fact that we are nothing more and nothing less than part of nature leads us to a better understanding of what we are and how the phenomena that affect us occur. This understanding is a great aid because it is based on a worldview much more adjusted to reality than the old beliefs, which lead us to unsolvable conflicts if we dare to reason about them.

We can face the big questions, make sense of our lives and understand ourselves by accepting that there is no god, no soul, no self and no free will. I think that in this way life is much more fascinating to us and we can adapt better to reality than with the old beliefs that shaped our vision of the world.

This book is the result of applying what I have learned from scientists and philosophers to different aspects of life. At the end of the book there is a guide for direct access to that information.

If you would like to leave a comment, delve into the topics covered or simply check what is out there, you can visit **www.fascinaos.com** (be fascinated).

# I

BE FASCINATED!

# 1

## BE FASCINATED!

Billions of years ago, galaxies, stars and planets began to form... On at least one of those planets, a series of events gave rise to very simple organisms, which reproduced and increased in number, diversity and complexity.

After a few billions of years more, on this planet, a huge ball that travels through space spinning around an immense mass of burning gas, there are now millions of species of organisms. Phenomena such as thought, consciousness and communication take place in some of these species. And only one has developed writing, science, technology...

In an organism of this species, some thoughts have taken place, along with an intention to express them in written language. And employing a technology that makes it possible to instantly send information anywhere on this huge ball, these words are now being perceived many kilometers away by another organism, in which thoughts related to these written words are taking place.

No matter how you look at it, these facts—and many others—seem fascinating to me.

Being able to think, feel, speak, see, hear, walk and perform many other common actions in our daily lives is invaluable to us. Yet we do not appreciate enough how tremendously fortunate we are to be able to enjoy these capabilities.

It is obvious that not everything in life is peachy and that we face difficulties and distress to a greater or lesser extent. But unless we find ourselves in a dramatic or very complicated situation, I think we should expect to feel lucky and fascinated for so many reasons.

I believe that by sharing ideas, information and insights we can make our sensations and feelings more in step with the amazing reality of which we are a part.

# II

# WHY ARE WE NOT FASCINATED?

# 2

# WHY ARE WE NOT FASCINATED?

As we have seen, we are part of a mind-blowing reality; however, by and large, we are not astonished by it. What led us to this situation? How is it possible that our immense advance in knowledge does not lead us to be amazed at the so many wonders we have discovered?

One of the causes is that this knowledge currently coexists with disparate worldviews, which are a byproduct of the ancient explanations that our ancestors gave to natural phenomena with practically no knowledge about them. These explanations include ideas such as that the universe was created with a purpose by a god, or that we have a soul that lives eternally and that after this life we will have another "immaterial life" that will be wonderful or terrible as a reward or punishment, depending on if said god approves or disapproves of our behavior.

There are thousands of superstitions derived from these and other ideas that even today move many people away from the explanation of what we are: nothing more and nothing less than organisms made up of 50 trillion cells and 7,000 septillion atoms—we are part of the current state of the innumerable natural processes that we know deeply enough to discard all kinds of old superstitious beliefs.

Why do we not simply abandon those superstitions in order to better adapt to reality? Because along with those superstitions came fears and expectations that were installed in our worldview and are still deeply rooted in our society. The greater part of humanity continues to fear punishment from a god, karma, or some sort of "energy" if they do not follow the rules that some enlightened person has dictated. And they hope that, if they do follow them, they will one day receive that wonderful eternal life, or that better reincarnation, or nirvana, or they will "be one with the cosmos."

But the problem is not "just" that. In addition, those rules, based on tremendous ignorance, often have seriously harmful effects on those who believe in them and, unfortunately, also on those who do not believe in them. One of those effects is the fear of a god because he can punish you with the torments of hell "for your fault, for your most grievous fault." Other effects are sexual repression, indoctrination, tithing (still imposed in many places), homophobia, sexism (which in some religions reaches unbelievable extremes), submission from childhood to religious authority (to the point of confessing your "sins" to a man so that he imposes a penance and forgives you in the name of an absolute power) and a long etcetera.

Thus, all the fascination caused by the knowledge we have acquired fades when we fail to be consistent with the information we have, because the fears and hopes associated with our superstitions weigh us down and getting rid of them is an uphill battle. A very enlightening example of this is our attitude towards death:

We know that after death our consciousness ceases to exist and that the organism that we now are decomposes. The organism that we were no longer exists. Just like the chicken we ate. But we do not naturally accept this fact; we turn it into a taboo. Proof of this is that death, perhaps the event that causes us the most pain in our lives, does not deserve a second of attention in the twenty years that a person may spend in formal education. We do not spare a single minute to talk about it. This issue is only openly addressed in society from the standpoint of superstitious beliefs, which favors the continuity of these beliefs.

And not only do we leave aside very important issues such as death. We also commit the terrible mistake of promoting the idea that all beliefs must be respected, including the belief that if you deny the existence of a god you must suffer eternally for it. This idea may seem laughable to many, but even today it causes terrible suffering to millions of people.

Hence, we do not achieve all the peace, tranquility and happiness that we could by understanding that we are a wonderful organism in which amazing phenomena take place. Although we do not believe in old superstitions, we have not fully abandoned derivatives of them such as the belief in a kind of soul-like self, in some kind of abstract immortality, in transcendence, in free will, etc.

But when we are consistent with everything we know and accept reality as shown to us by science and other branches of knowledge, we begin to free ourselves from traumas, fears, repressions and distressing cognitive dissonances. And this allows us to move towards that peace, tranquility and happiness that ignorance did not allow us to achieve.

# FREE WILL AND THE SELF

Once we realize that there is no god, I believe that the next most important matter, by far, is to realize that the free will we thought we had does not exist, and that there is not even a self that could have free will to begin with.

It sounds like bad news, but it is not. Understanding this matter frees us from a lot of the suffering related to hatred, self-esteem, pride, shame, arrogance, mortifying repentance, the desire for revenge, disdain, judgment, humiliation, responsibility, guilt, forgiveness, merit, humility, duty, approval, control...

The matter is not as complicated as it sounds. Just like with the idea of a god, the problem understanding it is the incredible amount of confusing arguments, fallacies and shifts in meaning that have been presented, and the profound extent to which they have permeated our society.

For starters, let us define what we mean by *free will* and *self*.

"Free will is the supposed power or capacity of humans to make decisions or perform actions independently of any prior event or state of the universe." (*Encyclopedia Britannica*)

That is, an ability to make decisions or perform actions that are not just a consequence of natural phenomena configured by the previous conditions of the universe (including the organism), cause-effect relationships and/or randomness, and the different laws of nature. A capacity that "I" have because "I" have an organism. I am like a passenger in that organism; I do what "I" want with it; I am its owner and "I" govern it. And although uncontrollable phenomena occur in that organism which is "mine," other phenomena such as decisions and actions are created, configured and controlled by "me"—they are "my" decisions and actions. "I" create them.

We acknowledge that the digestion of food, the beating of the heart, the production of insulin, etc., are purely natural processes. "I" do not bring these things about, "they do so themselves." But I feel that "I" drive my thoughts, decisions and actions.

That "I"—the self—is what does not exist. That self is like a minigod presumed to inhabit every human organism. It is akin to a soul. It is not part of the purely natural world. We think we are something beyond the organism; more than a bunch of cells. That "thing beyond" is the self. And no, it does not exist.

The truth is that we are organisms, part of the matter that forms the universe. And everything that happens in the universe, both outside and inside our skin, are natural phenomena: they happen without there being "someone" to make them happen. No one rains, snows, or produces earthquakes. No one beats their heart, secretes insulin, or digests their food. Similarly, thoughts, desires, wills, decisions... are also natural phenomena that occur in the brain: there is "no one" to do all this either. There is no "digester" of food, no thinker and no decision-maker. There is no self, no agency (authorship) and no free will. These are concepts that do not have a correspondence with something real.

Several points lead to confusion:

As Stephen Wolfram explains, one of the reasons is our lack of understanding that systems based on the sum of many simple elements and rules give rise to phenomena of extreme complexity. To us, it seems that these complex systems are free of those simple elements and rules and that they are governed by "something else." Thus, we think that what happens in the brain cannot solely be the result of 86,000 million neurons and trillions of relationships between them. There must be something else...

Another reason is that we tend to give agency to the complex phenomena we observe. When we see a simple phenomenon, like a rock falling down a mountain, we understand that there is no one doing that. The rain and the lightning seemed more complicated to us and we indeed thought that someone did that (Zeus). Then we realized that it was also natural. We believed that some diseases such as epilepsy were caused by demons, but then we realized that they were natural. But thoughts, desires and actions are the last bastion of that agency, of that "someone." There must be someone at the wheel, some sort of minigod: the self.

Lastly, we often confuse perception with creation. Whenever we perceive that a thought, a desire, etc., appears in our brain, we have the feeling that we are creating that thought or desire. It is enough to pay close attention to our thoughts and desires to see that they appear "by themselves"—they manifest without us having absolutely any control or authorship over them.

In future chapters, we will continue to deal with this fundamental issue of free will and the self.

# 4

# THE FEAR OF DEATH

First of all, I should clarify that when we talk about the fear of death, we obviously mean the fear *of the idea* that life comes to an end. Do not confuse our survival instinct with the fear of death. It is a fact that thanks to our survival instinct we will try to avoid an accidental or violent death at all costs; and the fear of this way of dying is entirely natural, healthy and convenient. But when we talk about the fear of death we refer to the anguish at the idea that one day we will cease to exist.

You can live without the fear of death. Millions of people like me are doing it. If you have been lucky enough to have not been indoctrinated with any irrational beliefs, the idea of death may not trouble you. But many of us who grew up believing we were immortal have had to reflect on this for a long time before we were completely at ease with the idea that one day we will cease to exist. Once you have come to terms with it, you realize that understanding this is a great relief and that irrational beliefs may give you peace in the absence of reason, but they create a growing conflict as understanding develops. Understanding something as simple and obvious as the fact that we are going to die is essential to understanding reality, adapting to it and being happy.

Why do we fear death?

We would not exist without the instinct of survival. When phenomena such as consciousness and complex thinking arose, the idea of death must have surely been most disturbing to our ancestors. In fact, every culture has had a belief system that included some form of afterlife. It seems that we have been denying our death since we began to become aware of it. After millions of years of terrible and constant struggle trying to eliminate at all costs any chance of dying, when our understanding began to reveal the certainty of death, the revelation was too hard for us to accept.

Much has happened since then, but even today, as we saw in the chapter "Why are we not fascinated?", the taboo of death is so strong that a person can spend twenty years of education in school, college and university and not hear a single minute of conversation about death. The most important fact in our lives is not worth a single minute of attention in our education systems. Most people do not even want to hear about death and live in a constant flight from a problem that is ever-present. Every time someone dies or gets sick; every time we buckle up in the car or look before crossing the street; our day-to-day lives constantly remind us of this possibility.

Because of this lasting inability to accept the idea of death, most people hold on to the irrational beliefs they were indoctrinated with or conjure up new ones that, like any other form of ignorance, will have negative consequences; among them, cognitive dissonances—the clash between beliefs and reality. I once read a sentence that I have not been able to find again. It more or less said, "What if all of humanity's problems stemmed from not accepting the fact that we are going to die?" It struck me as an exaggeration, but at the same time, it caused such an impression that I remember it often. And, indeed, the fear of death is a source of many problems such as irrational beliefs, wasted resources, values and crucial concepts that are completely wrong or meaningless, and a very long etcetera that includes religion, one of whose fundamental pillars is precisely the fear of death. As a matter of fact, the first question that an atheist is usually met with is: "So, you die and that's it?"

Of course it is. Once you are at peace with the idea that one day you will disappear, you realize what great relief we were talking about. You realize that the idea of a god, eternal life or reincarnation actually created so much confusion for you because they are impossible; and, deep down, many believers know or suspect this. Faith is not certainty; it is invoked to try to justify this incongruity. But not only is it not certainty, it is fantasy. That is why it does not work. This explains why people who believe (or, rather, try to believe) in eternal life are not happier than those who do not entertain that fantasy, although it is to be expected that they should be much happier.

Luckily, more and more people understand the reality of death; but the taboo remains pervasive. The fear remains. Only when we finally dare to speak about death naturally and observe our life from a point of view adjusted to reality can we successfully adapt to it. When the fantasies of immortality are truly left behind us, death is as comprehensible as any other fact; and the fact that so many people talk about it as if it were complicated, mysterious or enigmatic is quite perplexing.

The first step to stop being afraid of death is to understand that there is actually nothing to fear. Amongst the ideas that lead us to such comprehension, one of the oldest is the one that Epicurus expressed with both overwhelming logic and poetic beauty: when death happens, you no longer exist. It is irrational to suffer for something that will happen "to you" precisely when you no longer exist. Fearing the possible pain before dying is reasonable (luckily, in developed countries and in most cases, this is something that nowadays has a solution). It also is reasonable to think about the sadness of those who survive us. It is even reasonable to think that we would like to live longer, as we would like many impossible things. But the fear of death itself, of ceasing to exist, is totally unfounded. You did not exist until a few years ago. The same problem you had then is what you will have in a few decades.

On a more practical level, understanding that without death we could not exist helps us to accept it and to also come to terms with it. The evolution of species, the need to use limited resources and many other natural phenomena lead us to realize that, were there no death, we could not be the organisms that we are—the result of evolution over billions of generations of deceased ancestors. Just like them, we are part of history. This is an idea that is more important than it sounds. It is not like our existence will somehow be erased when we die as if it never happened. Everything that we value today will have always existed. We will always be those beings who lived in this space and time.

On a more philosophical level, understanding the absence of a self can help us remove some of the added drama surrounding the idea of death. Our life is a series of natural phenomena that merely stop when we die. Understanding this reality is less dramatic than believing that there is a self, an essence that will somehow be lost. When we reflect on the absence of the self, we see ourselves as something that is intrinsically part of the universe, not as something separate from the world, a soul that inhabits a body or a self that governs it. Hence, it becomes less and less tragic that the very small part of the natural processes that are our life stops and that the immensity of the rest of them continues its course.

Coming to terms with the reality of death liberates us from a lot of suffering and makes us feel lucky for many reasons. One of them is that we realize the priceless value of our life. One of the serious problems of superstitious views is that they tend to belittle life by considering it simply a preliminary step before a supposed eternal life full of happiness. This is one of the things that make religions so useful in manipulating people. You can convince someone to accept harsh living conditions if you make them believe that infinite compensation awaits them afterwards. This is so absurd and sad that it is unbelievable that nowadays it still happens so often.

On the other hand, being aware that we have a limited life motivates us to make the most out of it. This is obvious; if you have a few decades to live you will manage your resources better than if you have "all eternity." That is why we have very good reasons to place great value on the proper management of time and resources, on minimalism (I would call it "worth-ism") and on all the information that helps us to be happier.

Another consequence of being aware that life has an end is that it becomes less difficult for us to come to terms with the death of the people we love. If we believe in eternal life, we find it so illogical that we spend our lives in doubt, avoiding certain thoughts and trying to deny the evidence that is continually presented to us. And when someone dies we are bewildered—we do not really start the process of grief; nor do we accept the facts; nor can we adapt to them. On the one hand, we think we should be happy because our loved one is with our god, or reincarnating, or whatever; and we see pain as a failure, something that should not happen. Not so intensely, at least. But on the other hand, these ideas are so absurd that almost no one actually believes them. More than a belief, it is a *failed attempt* to believe. We are in doubt, which does not let us accept the death of our loved one and live on in peace with our memories of them. Cognitive dissonance, the conflict between what a person believes and what they observe in reality, has devastating effects when people trying to believe in an eternal life face the death of a loved one.

As always, knowledge is what allows us to live without the conflicts and severe limitations of superstitious worldviews. Faced with any fact, however hard it may be for us, understanding what is happening is the first step that enables us to adapt to the situation in the best possible way. And the death of a loved one is one of the cases in which irrational beliefs carry the most suffering. If we do not try to deny the pain or disguise it with vain hopes, the whole grieving process takes place more healthily and it eases the adaptation to the new circumstances. With no taboos or a distorted reality, death does not catch us off guard. This may sound silly, but it is not. Faced with the death of someone close, or with the proximity of their own death, many people realize that they have spent their lives avoiding thinking about these issues and have a sudden and terrible clash with the reality from which they were constantly trying to flee.

The pain felt in the face of someone's death occurs because we have felt love for that person. That is something very valuable, and will continue to be. Everything we have experienced with that person is still part of us. The great pain caused by their absence is natural and it is better to live it without trying to deny it, avoid it, or disguise it. Accepting it and sharing it helps us to deal with the blow. The best help in grieving is the company and support of the people we care about. False illusions only hinder our understanding and undermine, delay or even prevent us from living the grieving process in a healthy way. This can lengthen the intense pain for much longer than would be expected. On the other hand, when we naturally accept the reality of death, the pain in the memory of the loved one decreases over time and combines with a mixture of nostalgia and happiness.

Understanding the reality of death also facilitates the solution to unnecessary suffering when life becomes unbearably painful: euthanasia or assisted suicide. All the reasons for not allowing them are absolutely irrational. Fortunately, more and more countries are legislating to allow this fundamental human right to a dignified death.

But the fear of death and all the superstitions around it are still very present in society today. That is why we must come forth and not be condescending to superstition and ignorance. We should talk about all of this whenever we can, with as much care and honesty as possible, to help people understand that freeing yourself from irrational beliefs makes you happier.

Unfortunately, the social pressure that compels us not to talk about death is very strong, especially when it comes to children. We think that children are not prepared to talk about this topic, which is a big mistake. If we cannot talk about something with a child, it is often because we do not completely understand it ourselves. Children have a great capacity to adapt to reality if we do not confuse them with false information. My personal experience in this regard was very revealing. My mother died when my son was about four years old. I said, "Grandma's dead." He replied, "Dead?" "Yes," I answered. At that moment, we only crossed those few words. A few days later, when we were in the car, he suddenly asked me, "And why did Grandma die?" So I explained in a very simple way that people get old and die. He did not ask me anything else, and that was it. Another day, also suddenly in the car, he told me, "Now I understand—when something is very old… if it is a toy it breaks, if it's a person, they die." It worked wonders to simply answer his questions in all sincerity. At his own pace, he soon grasped the subject of death. Often, when we do not know how to talk about something, simply trying to tell the truth produces surprisingly good results.

Last but not least, accepting death also allows us to understand that our existence does not "have a meaning," as we will see in the chapter "What is the meaning of life?" Many times we are taught that the meaning of our life is doing what a religion or some other modern superstition tells us to do to obtain the prize it promises us. That is why the victims of these deceptions think that without their god, paradise, or nirvana, they could not give meaning to their lives and often do not dare to think that their irrational beliefs could be a fantasy. Such is the fear of existential emptiness and a meaningless life. That is why it is a great relief to understand that we give meaning to our lives by knowing, sharing and caring for everything we consider valuable.

# 5

# SPIRITUALITY

The word *spiritual* means "of, pertaining to, or consisting of *spirit*." And the word spirit leaves little doubt as to what we mean: a soul, an immaterial being, etc.

Fortunately, in scientific, academic, or any other minimally serious fields, there is no longer talk of a soul or a spirit. This is relegated to religions and other irrational beliefs.

But some people want spirituality to be talked about everywhere and so have been inventing new meanings for the word *spiritual*. These meanings are already perfectly expressed in other words, but to try to ratify spirituality in all spheres, some now say that spirituality consists of things like love, the search for knowledge, solidarity, or art. That is false. These human values have nothing to do with belief in such things as a spirit.

Unfortunately, some public figures with scientific knowledge but also with irrational attitudes or beliefs join this unfortunate practice. And some people do not hold these beliefs, but, in a naive attempt to reconcile the irreconcilable, end up putting irrational beliefs and human values in the same bag.

The result of all this is a tremendous confusion that we must clarify—human values are one thing and spirituality is another.

Spirituality is a concept used in the realm of religions and similar beliefs. The fact that in these contexts human values such as generosity or solidarity are also discussed does not mean that these values are part of spiritual belief. Being generous or supportive does not at all imply that you "live a spiritual life."

Saying that spirituality consists of having values that have nothing to do with it is an attempt by people with spiritual beliefs to hijack these values and to force us all to admit that we are in some way spiritual. But people like us with a rational, critical, scientific and ethical view of life possess all the human values and do not believe in anything spiritual. There is nothing spiritual about our lives.

It is a serious mistake to accept the label *spiritual* for human values that have nothing to do with spiritual beliefs because this creates confusion that hinders communication and knowledge, which are pillars of the utmost importance in our lives.

# 6

# MINIMALISM

It is very common to meet people whose lives are so overloaded that they do not have the opportunity to spend time calmly reflecting on the issues we are dealing with here. For this and other reasons, minimalism is a very valuable and necessary concept in modern life.

First of all, we must clear up this confusion: minimalism is not exactly about having as few things as possible. It consists of investing our resources (time, wealth, space, energy...), of which we never have a surplus, in what we consider valuable. I think a more precise name would be "worth-ism" or "rational use of resources."

The concept of minimalism can be applied in all fields of life: things we buy or own, time we spend on different activities, the size of our house, etc.

We all have many things that we do not use and that take up a lot of space. We also spend a lot of time, money and energy on activities, relationships and commitments that are not valuable to us. It seems that almost no one has free time, especially for what they would really like. Time is the most precious resource we have. We cannot increase it; we have what we have.

What we can drastically increase is our well-being, eliminating what is least valuable to us and using the resources we have freed up for the first thing on our "waiting list." For this, we must be able to say "no" to everything that is not as important as what we want to include in our life. For example, we can stop spending time on activities of little value and use that time for that friend with whom we like to chat so much.

Nowadays, with the impressive technology available, our ability to obtain anything has multiplied incredibly: information, social contacts, participation in activities, food, clothes, books, music, videos... The great challenge we face is to choose what we consider most valuable. If we feel overwhelmed by such abundance, we need to be a little more minimalist and we can start in many ways:

- Before doing anything, we should assess whether it will actually be valuable to us. This way we will immediately reduce the excess of things in our way.

- We can start saying "no" to what we used to say "yes" before out of commitment or habit.

- We can get rid of things that we do not use or that do not really have value for us. We can start by giving away or throwing away what occupies space unnecessarily. Soon we will see the amount of free space we have left and the time we will no longer waste in managing that entire surplus we had.

- We can stop spending time in social relationships or situations that do not make us feel good and actively start creating situations that are interesting to us.

- We can stop shopping as an activity and only go shopping when we have a need or a desire for something we find valuable.

- We can reduce the number of gifts we give because of a certain date or commitment.

- In short, whenever possible, we can eliminate what is not valuable and use the resources we have freed for what is.

A common mistake regarding many attitudes such as minimalism is to think that it is a binary question—either you are a minimalist or you are not. This is not true. We are all minimalists to some extent. Sooner or later, everyone reaches a limit regarding the resources they are willing to invest in something. The problem is that this limit is usually too high for many things that we do not consider valuable.

Another mistake is to consider that minimalism has something to do with selfishness or with stinginess. It absolutely does not. In fact, the time or wealth we spend helping someone is almost always extremely valuable to us.

What, then, is the ideal state of our life in terms of the rational use of our resources? The one in which most of them (time, money, space...) are occupied in what we consider most valuable and, moreover, in which we still have resources available for what might come up.

Keep in mind that, as always, when we adopt an attitude that is not shared by the majority of people, to some extent we are going to face the rejection of a large part of society. As Mario Benedetti said, "Being free is not for everyone. You have to have the courage to lose face in the eyes of many people, say goodbye to many others and be ready to be hated." This quote may seem a bit exaggerated when talking about minimalism. But try to start saying no to what is not of value to you (invitations to boring social meetings, events that you find uninteresting, buying lotteries, giving gifts out of a sense of obligation...) and you will see that the quote is not overstated at all.

This social rejection might seem negative, but over time we learn that it indeed helps us realize which social relationships are worthwhile. Besides, the consequences of minimalism in our lives are spectacularly good:

- We have more money available.

- In the long run, therefore, we need to work less.

- We are less caught up in unwanted social gatherings.

- We have more time, money, space and availability for what really matters to us and makes our lives better.

- Our social life improves considerably: if a friend wants to chat with us, we will always have the available time. That is what I consider being rich to be.

# III

# THE BIG QUESTIONS

## WHO ARE WE?

In our daily lives, asking "who" has a very simple and practical function: to know which specific person we are referring to (e.g., "Who is coming home today?").

But if we are talking about our nature, about our existence, asking about who we are does not seem to make much sense. The question "who" is closely related to the idea of a self or an agency that, as we have seen, does not exist. What we are actually asking ourselves is *what* we are. And nowadays we have more than enough answers to understand it satisfactorily and to tremendously increase our knowledge about ourselves too: we are organisms made up of trillions of cells and septillions of atoms. We are part of the vast array of natural processes occurring in the universe. We are not something independent. We are part of what we call nature, exactly like everything that exists. We are made up of the same matter or energy that makes up everything that exists.

Our knowledge, both of what we are and of the universe in general, has increased dramatically in recent decades and it does not look as if it is going to stop; quite the opposite. This gives us many reasons to be joyful:

One of them is that we can very satisfactorily broadly appease our need to know what we are with relatively little effort.

Another great reason is that we can delve as much as we want into the knowledge of what we are and of the world of which we are a part. In this age of the Internet, we have an enormous amount of easily accessible information and more than enough of it to spend our whole lives enjoying the acquisition of more.

We also have the thrill of being alive in this historical moment in which knowledge advances most rapidly. We have been living in that moment constantly for many decades now, since the speed at which we learn has only increased, and does so ever more rapidly.

But the greatest reason for joy, the one that really changes our lives the most (and also, paradoxically, the most unknown and unappreciated), is that our knowledge not only gives us the delight of learning and understanding. It also boosts our well-being far more dramatically than most people realize. Interestingly, one of the bits of knowledge that most increase our well-being is precisely knowing how to use all kinds of our resources, including knowledge itself, as we saw in the chapter on minimalism, and will see again in the conclusions at the end of this book.

# 8

# WHERE DID WE COME FROM?

Most of the atoms that form us come from stars that no longer exist. We literally come from the stars. Once the planet Earth was formed, it was here where processes took place that led to the formation of the first simple organisms, our very first ancestors, and the countless generations of increasingly complex organisms, until we reached the millions of species that currently populate the planet.

Fascinating phenomena such as the emergence of consciousness, thought and communication took place in some of these organisms. And in the human species, we arrived at the incredible knowledge that we can share today thanks to the spectacular development of technology. We came from the stars and thus we have become what we are.

# 9

## WHERE ARE WE HEADING?

For the time being, we are still on Earth, but already there are always some people in the nearest region of space—on the International Space Station. Soon, there will always be someone on the Moon too, and we will probably reach Mars in the coming decades. From then on, it seems that we will have to wait a long time before going any further. And one day it will be necessary to do so, when the Sun grows and swallows the Earth. But there is no rush; that will take about five billion years. Who knows if by then any of our descendants or those of other species will remain and what they will be like?

But the question of where and how we are going to be able to survive here, on Earth, in the coming decades, is one of the great challenges that we are facing right now. This issue is certainly pressing. The misuse of increasingly powerful technologies and the exaggerated consumption of resources of all kinds threaten our well-being, our permanence on a great part of the planet and our very existence in ways that we do not even fully understand.

Decisive events will occur in the near future which we are speeding towards. The knowledge about the situation and the measures to be taken must urgently get to as much of humanity as possible. Soon we will be heading towards a setback in our well-being and unprecedented disasters, or towards the continuation of progress, the overcoming of difficulties, and a well-being that could surpass everything known so far. One of those two possibilities is where we are heading for.

# 10
# WHAT HAPPENS AFTER DEATH?

This is the easiest "big question" to answer—after death, the corpse decomposes. Jokes aside, if we do not hold irrational beliefs, this is not even a "big question" at all. It is like asking what happens after a fire goes out. The series of processes that was the fire has come to an end. Nothing "happens" after a bonfire is extinguished. Similarly, death is the end of a series of processes that took place in an organism. Nothing "happens" after death, either.

A very nice and also realistic idea about what happens after death is that our atoms become part of other things; even other living beings. But that romantic and beautiful idea is also a reality throughout our lives. We can now enjoy the feeling caused by knowing that this is already happening. Every day, we exchange so many atoms with our environment that there are already hundreds of kilograms of matter scattered around the world that once were part of you.

However, the question about what happens after death refers to how we will continue to exist, what will become of us after we die and how our thoughts and our consciousness will have continuity. If we have any doubts about "what happens after death" in this sense, it is because we still somehow believe that there must be something like a soul. Perhaps we do not believe in a god, or a heaven or a hell, but we still believe in the possibility of a kind of immaterial self.

When we truly accept that we are an organism and that there is no self or any kind of immaterial entity that inhabits it in any way, asking "what happens after death" ceases to make sense; just like asking what happens when the fire is extinguished. Life is a series of processes that occur in an organism. Death is the end of those processes. And when a process ends, nothing "happens"; the only thing that happens is, precisely, that this process has stopped occurring.

# 11

# WHAT IS THE MEANING OF LIFE?

This question usually refers to a purpose or a goal. We seem unwilling to accept that neither our own existence nor that of the universe has any purpose or goal.

For something to have a purpose, we need another element with respect to which that initial something has the purpose. For example, if we build a chair, we do it with the purpose of someone finding it useful by sitting on it, to get money in exchange for that chair, etc. But when we ask ourselves the purpose of something in itself, without referring to something else, we are asking an incoherent question. It is even more incoherent if we ask ourselves about the purpose of everything that exists as a whole, the universe, because in this case there cannot even be another element with respect to which it could have a purpose, since the universe is, by definition, everything that exists.

That is why whoever speaks of a purpose of our existence, or that of the universe, usually does so in reference to a god, an immaterial life after life, or something of the sort. This is why when you tell someone that the god they believe in does not exist, they usually reply, "So you die and that's it? In that case, life would be meaningless." And indeed it is. Life is a set of phenomena that takes place in the universe. And, like everything else in the universe, it does not exist because of a purpose, an intention, a goal, or anything like that. Purposes, intentions and goals are some of the ways in which ideas or concepts are related in some brains. Before those brains existed, there was no intention, purpose or goal. Asking about the meaning, purpose, intention or goal of our life's existence is just as incoherent as asking what things were called before we gave them names.

At this point, it is very useful to understand the process that has given rise to our existence—the evolution of species. Understanding the most elementary concepts of evolution leaves no doubt about the possible purpose of our existence: it is a totally incoherent idea. We have not been designed or created. Our configuration, like that of all that exists, is the outcome of an immense array of natural processes with no ultimate intention or purpose.

But, unfortunately, another of the very serious failures of our education system, along with not addressing the issue of death, is that, after many years of academic training, most people still do not understand, even in a simple way, biological evolution. Thus, although the idea that biological evolution occurs with some purpose is totally absurd, it is still believed by many more people than one might think.

As stated previously, purposes, intentions and goals are some of the ways in which ideas or concepts are related in some brains. Since this happens in our brains, questions about what meaning we give to the things we do in our lives are very useful and necessary. For these questions, we actually *can* find many answers and many purposes that are valuable to us. But to insistently seek what is the meaning, or purpose, of our existence itself is a way to waste time at best, or to reach a painful existential crisis at worst. And to believe in a religion, or in someone who tells us that the supposed purpose of our existence is to follow his orders and give in to his threats, are serious mistakes with dire consequences which most of humanity still makes.

What, then, are the purposes or the meanings we give to what we do in life?

Well, much of what we do, if not all, we do to satisfy our biological, psychological and social needs. Amongst the actions we undertake for this reason, I believe that three simple and noteworthy concepts are very present in almost everything that helps us make sense of what we do in our lives: to know, to share and to care. If we examine what aspects of our lives we find valuable, we will find that they very often include, in a very broad sense, these three actions. Let us consider:

TO KNOW:

We need to know the reality around us in general, and also know ourselves as part of it. We need to know our fellow human beings and relate to them in many ways.

TO SHARE:

A human being cannot survive alone. We need to share everything, from language, manners, values and the most abstract ideas, to all kinds of material resources. We are hyper social beings, and communicating and sharing with one or many people virtually every aspect of our lives is vital to our well-being.

TO CARE:

We need to feel that we are part of a community (from one that includes our family and friends to humanity as a whole), and to strive for the well-being of that community is a purpose that makes us perceive our life as something very valuable.

If something in our life includes these three concepts, it almost certainly helps us give value and meaning to what we do in life. And vice versa, if something helps us give value and meaning to what we do in life, it usually includes these three concepts in their broadest sense.

As an example, something as seemingly foreign to these ideas as chess, clearly includes these three actions. We need to know the rules and strategies, share the game with someone and take the utmost care in our execution to offer our opponent and ourselves a beautiful and valuable experience.

## 12

## FREEDOM AND FREE WILL

Barely anyone has a very clear idea of what "free will" means, and it is often confused with freedom.

Freedom is the ability to do what one wants to do. I can act according to my will. No one disputes that. The question is whether that will is "free."

We understand what the will is—to want something. Whether we can choose a certain option or another is not in question. The information that must sink in is that this will, this desire to choose "A" and not "B," is a natural phenomenon and, therefore, is configured by the previous conditions of the universe (us included), the relationship of cause and effect and randomness, and the different forces of nature.

To choose something, we must have a preference beforehand. And to choose to have such a preference is impossible. How can someone decide to have a preference? Do you make a list of possible preferences and then pick one? Why that one? Is it because of *another* previous preference? And why did you choose to have *that* one? And so on, absurdly, ad infinitum.

If you do not believe this, try changing a preference of yours. Of course, you could choose an apple when you in fact prefer a pineapple, in an attempt to show that your will is free. Big mistake. You had two desires and could only satisfy one: to eat pineapple or to try to prove that your will is free. And you chose the second one. But your preference for trying to prove that your will is free just happened in your brain, naturally. Too bad about the pineapple you did not enjoy.

Are we free, then? Yes, assuming that we are not imprisoned, bound, etc. When we ask if we are free, we clearly mean to be free from threats, pressures, imprisonments, etc.

Is our *will* free? First, we should know what it could be free *of*. Can our will even be free of something? When we want something, is there anything from which that wanting can be free? Can a desire, a natural phenomenon, be free? The idea of a free will is incoherent and absurd to this extent.

Asking whether there is free will is like asking whether there is free digestion. Both are natural phenomena, no matter how complicated or simple they may be.

We are free to do what our will leads us to do. But our will is shaped by multiple factors over which there is absolutely no control. If we lock a person in a room, they are not free to go wherever they want. When we open the door, nothing stops them anymore. That is to have freedom; in this case of movement, of action.

Let us say that person, now free, chooses to go and see their friend. The thought, desire and decision to go and see their friend is the result of events in their neurons and many other factors over which there is no control at all. That person has been able to go and see their friend freely (there is no locked door), but their preference, their willingness to go see their friend, has occurred naturally and is therefore shaped by causes, circumstances, etc.

There is a lot of confusion on this issue. Here are some examples:

One can think, "I want to eat a lot, but I don't because I know it's not healthy. That shows that I have free will." It absolutely does not. That shows that you have two desires: to eat a lot and to be healthy. It is impossible to satisfy both so you choose one, the one you prefer. You cannot prefer the other one. And that preference was not "created" by you; it was not created by anyone. It occurs naturally.

Another very common mistake is to conflate the change of opinions, plans, beliefs, etc., with having free will. All these changes have been produced by natural phenomena. New factors have appeared; new information and new circumstances inside and/or outside the brain. There is no control. Try to change your mind about something. Or when you do indeed change it, try to change it back to your previous opinion.

Many people believe that accepting that there is no free will is to degrade the concept of being human. That is absolutely false. It is simply leaving behind another belief in something unreal. It is, once again, to realize that we are part of nature and that the laws of nature do not change within our skin.

All this knowledge does not affect our freedom in any way. On the contrary, like all knowledge, it increases our capacity to make decisions that are more coherent with reality; more effective and more useful.

Freedom consists in the ability to do what we want: to act according to our will. It is a very important value for all of us. We can have freedom or not, depending on factors that limit our capacity for action, threaten us, etc. That our will is a natural phenomenon is a completely different matter. Therefore, it is not even possible to imagine what it could be free of. There is no control over our desires. This is something we can prove right now, trying not to want something that we do want.

# 13

# FREE WILL AND THE SELF: A SETTLED QUESTION?

There is a broad consensus regarding the facts: a large majority of scientists and philosophers do not believe in the self we are talking about, or in free will—that supposed ability of human beings to make decisions or perform actions regardless of any previous event or state of the universe. The accepted idea is that decisions and actions are natural phenomena configured by the previous conditions of the universe (including the organism), cause-effect relationships and/or randomness, and the different forces of nature. This chapter is an explanation of the shameful and spurious debate that is taking place nowadays about whether free will exists or not.

Those who try to maintain a debate do so by misrepresenting the meaning of the term *free will*. They say, "It is true that what has always been called *free will* does not exist, but from now on we are going to label something else as 'free will': to act according to our desires and not by coercion." Welcome to the bewildering world of compatibilism.

Compatibilism, the most regrettable part of the alleged debate, basically consists in admitting that free will does not exist. "However," it states, "since we supposedly need something to call 'free will'," for reasons that we will see later, "from now on we call *freedom* 'free will'"; that is, to be able to act according to our desires and not by coercion.

But the nonsense does not end there: compatibilism concedes that natural laws entail that a person cannot choose something other than what they choose, because natural laws determine their thoughts, wills and actions. That is, you have free will to choose the only option that natural laws determine that you choose. And compatibilists argue that as long as no one points a gun at you or anything forces you, if you do what you want to do, you have free will. No. That is not free will. That is freedom. Everyone knows this and there has never been any debate about it.

Freedom is being able to do your will. But the will is not "free," it is configured by factors over which there is no control. "We are free to do what we want but not to want what we want," as the philosopher Baruch Spinoza said.

That this absurd and false debate survives never ceases to amaze me, more so when the ridiculousness of compatibilism can be appreciated in its entire splendor; your will is free, but it is always directed to the only option that natural laws relentlessly determine.

Compatibilists have elaborated many definitions for free will, each one more surprising than the previous. For example, at 3:25 of the video "Daniel Dennett - What is *free will?*", on the *YouTube* channel *Closer To Truth* (the 6-minute one; there are two videos with that name), Dennett defines *free will* as "our capacity to see probable futures—futures that seem like they are going to happen—in time to take steps so that something else happens instead." This is something that no one has ever doubted that human beings can do, as often happens with the definitions of free will proposed by compatibilists.

It is easy to understand that being free means being able to *do* what you want, and free will means being able to choose what it is that you want; to choose what you want to want; to choose what you choose to want... The concept is absurd and incoherent no matter how you look at it. For example, you are free to choose chocolate or vanilla ice cream, but you are not free to want chocolate or vanilla. And tricks like choosing vanilla (when you like chocolate more) to try to prove that the will is free are obviously ridiculous—you could not choose to want to prove something.

Asking whether there is free will is like asking whether there is free digestion. Both are natural phenomena and are shaped by processes and factors over which there is no control.

How is it possible, then, for such an absurd and spurious debate to be taking place? Because there are always people who resist accepting the consequences of every dethronement of the human being, and they want to deny or disguise the undeniable: we are part of nature and the same laws govern outside as inside our skin.

And why would anyone want to prolong that debate?

One reason is that many compatibilists believe that society would collapse if the population stopped believing in free will. That we would have to empty the prisons and cancel all mortgages; that no one would be responsible for anything... This nonsense is spouted by Daniel Dennett, probably the most famous compatibilist alive.

This reminds us of the idea that without belief in a god, society would be chaotic; an extremist view happily refuted in many countries.

Also, many compatibilists believe that people will become depressed or confused when they come to know that there is no free will. And they try to avoid this alleged confusion by calling *freedom* "free will," which precisely is the cause of confusion and hinders the understanding of this most important issue. "One often meets his destiny on the road he takes to avoid it." (*Kung Fu Panda*)

Finally, they believe that all other consequences of knowing that there is no free will are bad. In future chapters, we will see that these consequences could not be better or more fascinating.

# THE DILEMMA BETWEEN DETERMINISM AND FREE WILL

Determinism asserts that "all events in the universe, including human decisions and actions, are causally inevitable. Determinism entails that, in a situation in which a person makes a certain decision or performs a certain action, it is impossible that they could have made any other decision or performed any other action. In other words, it is never true that people could have decided or acted otherwise than they actually did." (*Encyclopedia Britannica*)

The dilemma between determinism and free will is a false dilemma, as we shall see. But first, it is important to mention another very frequent and serious error. Often times we talk about the mentioned dilemma by equating it with the question, "Are we free or is everything determined?" This mistake of speaking about freedom and free will as if they were the same thing only adds even more confusion to that already created by the false dilemma. As we have seen in the chapter "Freedom and free will," they are two different things.

Returning to the dilemma in question, it is obvious that, if determinism is true, there can be no free will, since what we do is determined down to the last detail by previous conditions and causes. But it is a mistake to think that, therefore, free will can exist if determinism is false. Just because chance, randomness, happenstance, or any other factor over which there is no control can influence some decisions or actions does not mean that the will is "free." That the will is directed to where natural laws determine, or where natural laws determine in combination with chance, makes no difference as to whether it could be "free." Again, free of what?

On the other hand, the possibility of some indeterminacy, chance or randomness in the way in which events occur, and that "history is not written in advance," does not make free will less of an incoherent concept. It is impossible to even describe what it is, as we are seeing.

# 15

# VOLUNTARY AND INVOLUNTARY ACTIONS

Believing that if the will is not free there is no difference between voluntary and involuntary actions is a very frequent mistake.

Of course there are distinctions. In a voluntary action there are, as well as the perceptions and movements required to perform the action, other phenomena such as intention, reflection, deliberation, etc., that are not there in involuntary actions. And that difference is extremely important, especially when considering the consequences and possible implications of those actions. If someone kills a person as part of a plan, we face a very different problem than involuntary manslaughter. The consequences and the ideal measures to be taken will also be very different.

By definition, a voluntary action is one in which the will intervenes. What changes our understanding is knowing that this will is not created by a self, but rather is the result of complicated processes, causes and conditions (including possible randomness) and that it is totally configured by them. But there is no doubt that voluntary and involuntary actions exist.

What no one can do is decide in which direction their will goes. We do not choose to reach the conclusions we reach. We do not choose to believe what we believe. We do not choose to desire what we desire. Not only can we easily verify this in practice by trying to change our conclusions, beliefs or desires and then reversing the changes, but we can also see that it is difficult for us to even imagine how we could *do* any of these things. As philosopher Sam Harris says, "The concept of free will is so incoherent that it is hard to even imagine how it could exist."

# IV

## WHAT CHANGES ONCE YOU KNOW THERE IS NO SELF OR FREE WILL?

# 16

# WHAT DO WE DO ONCE WE UNDERSTAND THERE IS NO SELF OR FREE WILL?

Well, it turns out that we do not "do" anything. Now we know that there is no self that does anything. In fact, there is no "someone" who "does" anything. Everything that happens inside and outside our body is nothing more than events configured by previous causes and conditions.

Practically speaking, so that everyone understands, we continue to do what our nature leads us to do.

Many things change with this new knowledge, but there is no "me" that has to "do" anything about it. Some thoughts, desires and actions will simply be different from now on. But this is something that has already happened countless times, every time we learn something.

What did we do when we understood that there was no god? We "did" nothing; however, many of our thoughts, desires and actions were configured differently thereafter because we realized the nonexistence of the god we believed in. We thought that lightning was created by Zeus and then we understood that it was produced naturally, without "someone" to produce it. That changed our way of understanding and acting regarding lightning and everything in general. The same thing happens with the nonexistence of free will and the self.

What we thought before—especially in practical terms—was, "My body is like a car that has some kind of driver: 'me,' the self." Now we know that "my organism" is not "my" organism. There is no duality between an organism and its owner; I AM an organism. The idea of a self is a simplified model of reality that, like many others (the idea of a god, for example), has been generated in certain parts of that organism in which the perception and processing of information take place. Just like we stopped attributing the authorship of events to a god when we understood that there is none, we no longer attribute what happens in us to that self, to that driver. When we stopped believing in a god and dedicated ourselves to studying nature (including ourselves), without the distortion of reality or the cognitive dissonances that belief in gods implied, our effectiveness in understanding natural processes improved tremendously.

Similarly, ceasing to believe in the illusions of the self and free will gives us a better understanding of who we are and how it can increase our well-being in many ways. For decades, scientists have been giving us information about an enormous amount of knowledge, obtained through experiments, studies and conclusions, as foreign to the ideas of a self and free will as to any other unfounded idea such as gods, magic or the supernatural.

Just as physics and other sciences advance totally oblivious to the idea of a god who governs the universe, the sciences that study the human organism advance rapidly without a trace of that self or that free will that is as incoherent as it is inconceivable: one cannot explain what that free will can be free of, nor even articulate a coherent idea about what such a thing is.

The confusion on this subject is the same as on other occasions—we believe that certain phenomena occur because there is someone who causes them, an author. And when we are aware of a thought, a desire, or the execution of an action, we have a sense that something in us, a self, has *created* that thought, desire, or executed the action. But these thoughts, desires and actions occur because of a very complex series of events that take place in our brain. No one creates them, just as no one creates lightning. Our perplexity at these facts is the same as when we stop believing in a god and ask ourselves, "Who made all of this, then?" Then we answer to ourselves, "Obviously, no one did."

And there actually is no "someone." Just as no one "rains," no one creates any phenomena. Everything happens naturally, with no authorship. Both outside and inside our skulls. This is the crux of the matter: understanding that everything works the same outside our skulls as it does inside them. We are part of nature and the same laws govern outside and inside our skulls. This idea can be overwhelming at first. The selves that we thought existed are only mental constructs. But we have not lost anything. We lose the same thing we lost when we found out that there was no Zeus to throw lightning. That is, nothing. On the contrary, we got rid of an idea that only hindered our understanding, and then we began to understand how lightning happens.

In short, when we understand that neither free will nor the self exist, we do exactly the same thing as with any new knowledge we acquire—we simply take it into account; we are aware of it. And, like all knowledge, that of the nonexistence of the self and free will greatly influences—and in a very beneficial way—how our thoughts, desires, intentions and actions are produced.

# 17

## HATRED

Almost everyone, in some way, feels love for nature. We love the planet, the sea, the animals...

But hardly anyone hates anything that they consider natural. If a storm gets us wet, we do not hate the storm. If a mosquito bites us and transmits us a disease, we do not hate it.

This absence of hatred towards natural phenomena often includes human beings. If someone bumps into us when we turn a corner, we do not get angry or hate that person. This is not only in the case of involuntary actions. It also occurs in the case of voluntary ones if we understand that they have natural causes. That is why we do not hate people like Charles Whitman, an adorable young man who became a killer because of a brain tumor.

But when we cannot identify natural causes, we assume that thoughts, intentions and actions are created by "someone"—the self that governs an organism. And when any of these actions cause us harm, that gives rise to the hatred of that self governing the organism, an entity as nonexistent as Zeus, who threw lightning; or as Aeolus, who made the wind blow. The organism is what exists, not the self.

The keys to comprehend that this hatred makes no sense, nor has any rational justification, are:

1. Understanding that thoughts, intentions and actions are natural phenomena, whether caused by a tumor or by any other reason (events in our neurons, chemical reactions, etc.) and that—like everything that happens in the universe—they are "configured by previous conditions of the universe, the relationship of cause and effect and randomness, and the different forces of nature," as we saw in the chapter "Free will and the self."

2. Understanding that all this happens without there being "someone" who is authoring these events. It makes no sense to hate an organism for the natural phenomena that occur in it. And all the phenomena that occur in the universe, inside or outside organisms, occur without there being "someone" who authors them. When we hate, we hate the self we believe behind the wheel of an organism, creating the thoughts, intentions and actions. And no, there is no such self, as we also saw.

Among the events that shape our thoughts and feelings, how we perceive information is of tremendous importance. But a few minutes of reading about hatred or reflection on it are not enough for this information to cause a significant change in us. Misinformation about free will and the self has been influencing our brains all our lives. We probably need many hours of receiving and processing the right information for our thoughts and feelings to be consistent with the new information.

A great change occurs when this information is sufficiently understood: instead of hatred, any harmful actions trigger in our brains thoughts, intentions and actions that we believe can have beneficial effects, such as halting the organisms in which these phenomena occur or ensuring that the perception of the appropriate information occurs in them so that harmful intentions and thoughts are not triggered.

And the old reactions such as the desire for revenge, or the desire to harm the organism where phenomena that have caused us harm have taken place, give way to an understanding of the nature of those phenomena and a desire for actions to be taken to repair or lessen the damage, avoid possible future harmful actions, stimulate with the appropriate information the brain of the organism in question, promote changes in the way in which thoughts and intentions occur in it, etc.

This liberates us from the suffering caused by hatred, which can become as serious or even greater than the very harm that incited our hatred in the first place.

# 18

## WHY LOVE BUT NOT HATE?

A friend asked me a very interesting question regarding the chapter on hate, "How is it that knowing that there is no free will avoids hate, yet allows us to continue loving?"

I think this question assumes that love and hate are two poles of the same feeling, as heat and cold are of temperature. If we enjoy a warm atmosphere and the temperature begins to drop nonstop, we will surely be cold after some time.

But this does not happen with love and hate. Love and hate are like sweet and salty flavors: no matter how much we reduce the sweetness of food by decreasing sugar, we will never make it salty. To do this, we need another ingredient—salt. Similarly, when our love for someone diminishes for some reason, no matter how much our feelings turn away from love, there is nothing in that "direction" that necessarily leads us to hate that person. Something different must happen. Something that *incites* hatred.

As we saw in the previous chapter on hate, to hate someone we must believe in free will and the self. If we know they do not exist, we tend not to feel hatred.

However, to love someone we do not need these beliefs. Knowing that someone does what they do because that is their nature and it cannot be otherwise does not affect our feeling. Knowing that when someone is happy to see us they are so in a natural and spontaneous way does not take anything away from our love for that person.

We do not stop loving anyone just because they cannot help being attracted to us or because their feelings, which they cannot create or control, do not allow them to simply leave and abandon us. In fact, if we thought that they were able to leave at any given moment, effortlessly end our relationship and be happy, we would not feel loved. Similarly, we cannot choose to stop loving a person. Nor can we choose to love someone, no matter how painful the consequences of loving or not loving are.

What is more, understanding that what we do not like about a person we love is also something natural and not the doings of a self, helps us to be sympathetic without "blaming" the person for being the way they are (we will talk about guilt later).

You can live your life loving a lot and not hating at all. But not because we follow some commandment, we are offered a reward, or we are threatened with punishment. That is all absurd. No one can choose to love or hate, even if someone orders them to, or even tortures them. It is impossible.

# 19

## MERIT AND PRAISE

According to the Royal Academy of Spanish Language, merit is "the right to recognition, praise, etc., due to the actions or qualities of a person." Praise is "expressing appreciation or admiration for something or someone, highlighting their qualities or their merits."

When we clearly understand that there is no self or free will, the meaning we give to this recognition is simply to share our joy with the person in question because we appreciate and value those actions or qualities. This starts a virtuous circle of good feelings: we consider ourselves lucky to enjoy something and, by sharing it with others, we feel increasingly happy to see how others enjoy and share it.

We can see many examples in which this happens, not because the people involved do not believe in the self or free will, but because they do not take them into account in those situations. For example, when we take someone to be very intelligent and we enjoy listening to them talk, we let them know, and this causes that virtuous circle of good feelings I mentioned. In this case, we are aware that he is very intelligent because "he was born that way."

But our concept of merit is more often attributed to those actions or qualities that are the result of effort. And, although motivation, resistance to fatigue and any other condition necessary to achieve something with effort are also the result of natural processes, we are more prone to the intuition that they are caused by a self with its free will. When we understand that this is not the case, we see that we can continue to appreciate these features as we did with intelligence. Following the previous example, we could say, "It is great that you not only are very intelligent, but you also have traits that make it possible for you to work intensively and constantly—you have studied a lot and now you can teach us many things."

On the other hand, attributing any good action to a self and its free will is a mistake that can lead us to think that there is something in that self that makes it more valuable than other selves; that there is something superior in its will above others that, being equally free, are not directed towards similar objectives. This mistake can also lead us to the deification of people with certain characteristics and to feelings of superiority or inferiority, arrogance, disdain, humiliation, low self-esteem, etc., which will hardly occur if we see everything that happens as natural phenomena.

# 20

# PRIDE, ARROGANCE AND DISDAIN

According to the Oxford Dictionary, these words mean the following:

**Pride:**
1. "A feeling of deep pleasure or satisfaction derived from one's own achievements, the achievements of those with whom one is closely associated, or from qualities or possessions that are widely admired."
2. "A high opinion of one's own worth or importance which gives rise to a feeling or attitude of superiority over others; inordinate self-esteem."

**Arrogant:**
"Having or revealing an exaggerated sense of one's own importance or abilities."

**Disdain:**
"The feeling entertained towards that which one thinks unworthy of notice or beneath one's dignity."

As we can see, these three concepts are closely related to each other. Of all these definitions, probably the first one of pride is the only one that refers to something good and appropriate. It is very reasonable to feel "satisfaction derived from one's own achievements, the achievements of those with whom one is closely associated, or from qualities or possessions that are widely admired." But when we attribute the merit to a self with free will, it is very easy to believe that such self is in itself superior to others who cannot do the same. This will likely cause the other attitudes described in the definitions. We often feel superior or inferior to people with abilities different from our own.

Moreover, achieving with effort something for which certain abilities have been necessary can also lead to a feeling of superiority. And this often leads to a feeling of inferiority in other people, even if the lucky person is not proud or arrogant. Merely seeing that someone achieves something that we cannot achieve makes us feel inferior because we think that the self that governs that organism has achieved that result thanks—at least in part—to its free will. We would like to obtain that result, but we blame our self for not using its free will as it should, as the lucky person did.

These problems do not usually occur if we clearly understand that when someone enjoys any ability or obtains some good result from their actions, it is because they have been lucky enough about the circumstances that have made it possible, both outside and inside their brain.

When we are aware that any capacity or attribute we have, as well as the actions we undertake and their consequences, are the result of natural processes, we can obtain the mentioned "feeling of satisfaction" about all this in a healthy way; one that does not imply any feeling of superiority, arrogance or disdain towards anyone.

## HUMILITY

According to the Royal Academy of Spanish Language, humility is a virtue that consists of knowing one's own limitations and weaknesses and acting according to this knowledge.

According to the Oxford Dictionary, "He is humble who has or shows a modest or low estimate of one's importance."

According to Wikipedia, the humble person can downplay their achievements and virtues and recognize their flaws and mistakes.

We can see that, again, accepting the nonexistence of the self and free will brings along these concepts of humility from the outset. We can hardly fall for pride, vanity or conceit (the opposite of humility), if we acknowledge that we are organisms in which natural phenomena take place.

But it is often said that to affirm the nonexistence of the self and free will is to degrade the human being. I do not see how describing reality degrades anything. What happens is that said realization—that we are simply part of nature—eliminates the last redoubt of that feeling of superiority of the human being with respect to the rest of what exists. We discovered that the universe was not created for us, that the Earth is not the center of the universe, that we are not immortal and that no god told us to "be fruitful, and multiply, and replenish the earth, and subdue it." Lastly, we are discovering that no self governs the organism, nor governs the supposed free will that such a self directed to where it desired.

What is left, then? We are left with what actually has been making the difference between suffering and well-being for as long as we can remember—knowledge. The more we learn about our traits and about all the processes that affect us, the less suffering and the more well-being of all kinds will exist in our lives. When we understand that we are nothing more and nothing less than part of the amazing nature, of the fascinating universe, we feel at peace and integrated in the world of which we are part.

## 22

## SELF-ESTEEM

If you have read this far, you probably already imagine that the concept of self-esteem is going to change drastically. In fact, in a way, it is going to disappear entirely. And, just as with the understanding of other implications of the nonexistence of free will and the self, this change will grant us a well-being that we cannot achieve while we believe that we have a self that governs certain aspects of our life with its free will.

Indeed, the concept of self-esteem is linked to the belief in the self and loses its entire role in our lives when we understand the nonexistence of this self. So, the question, "Do you have high or low self-esteem?" makes as little sense to us as, "Do you have much or little fear of God?"

Let us consider:

A person can feel discontent, or even very sad, because, in some of their organs, some circumstances cause them to lack a greater well-being. But that does not lower their self-esteem. All available arrangements are simply made to achieve the greatest well-being possible for them. For example, diabetes can be catastrophic for our quality of life. That is why medication, insulin, proper habits, etc., are used to minimize that loss of well-being. But since we know that diabetes is something that has happened naturally, that we did not create it, our self-esteem is not affected.

However, when the brain is that organ in which the circumstances that would cause greater well-being do not exist, we see everything differently. Because we think that we have a self which is the author of the thoughts and other events that occur in our brain, we feel that the self has created the circumstances that bring us discomfort and we evaluate it negatively—we believe that that "I" is not good enough; we have low self-esteem. Self-esteem is always directed towards that nonexistent self; never towards an organ of the organism that we are.

The brain is an organ in which events take place that, like the rest, are configured by previous causes, conditions, etc. Why is it, then, that what happens in our brain, causing us discomfort, provokes a problem in self-esteem? The cause is the erroneous belief that a self is the origin and therefore has done a bad job. We truly have the feeling that our thoughts, desires and behaviors are not natural phenomena that occur in our brain, but actions originated by a self with free will, which has not complied with what it should have done and, therefore, is guilty. Our self is guilty of doing things that make us feel bad. No one blames themselves for having diabetes, but they do blame themselves because their self has not used its free will to make them feel good. When we acknowledge that we are organisms without any governing self, we understand that it is just as absurd to blame a pancreas for diabetes as it is to blame a brain for a thought, a desire, or a behavior.

Imagine a human brain on a table. Is that piece of meat the culprit? Is it responsible for something that happened years ago? Of course not. Yet we think it *was* responsible when it was inside a living organism? It was obviously not, either.

So what is the solution to this whole problem about self-esteem? It is the same solution to all problems related to the belief in a self with free will. As a matter of fact, it is the same solution to all problems of any kind: learning as much as we can about the circumstances and events that have given rise to the situation that poses a problem to us, and put in place all the processes available to achieve the greatest well-being possible. In the case of the problem of self-esteem, the solution is understanding that our brain is an organ with no less than eighty-six billion neurons; a set of very complicated systems in which events occur—let us say it again—configured by previous causes, conditions, etc.

With this understanding, without the additional serious problem of underestimating our nonexistent self, without our "lack of self-esteem," we will be in a better position to improve our well-being. We will be able to better use all our resources, in addition to seeking the necessary help, to solve what causes us discomfort, whether it is diabetes, depression, anxiety, addiction, difficulty in establishing healthy habits, or any other situation.

Our brains form ideas, images and models of everything we perceive. This obviously includes the organism that we are. We have an image of ourselves. And the more that image is adjusted to reality, the more effective will be the processes that are put in place to improve our well-being. Thus, if the image we have of ourselves is that of an organism with a self, a driver who is responsible for what happens in it, we will be just as mistaken as those who blame natural phenomena on a god and get angry at it when those phenomena harm them. The internal conflict because that self does not get what we would like will appear again and again.

However, when the image we have of ourselves is that of an organism in which events take place (configured by causes, etc.), we will hardly have any problems with our self-esteem, because we understand that there is no self we may approve or disqualify.

# 23

# SHAME

Oxford Languages gives us two meanings of this word:
1. "The feeling of loss of dignity caused by a fault committed or by a humiliation or insult received."
2. "The feeling of discomfort produced by the fear of making a fool of oneself, or that someone will do so."

When we perform an action that harms someone, we often feel a discomfort that leads us to take action to repair the damage caused, as much as possible, and try not to let something similar happen again. However, the feeling that there is a loss of dignity implied does not make much sense. We did the only thing we could do. We accept that. We also accept the consequences of those actions and we do everything we can to improve the situation. This loss of dignity does not seem to us the consequence of natural phenomena that gave rise to a situation, but of the action of a self that with its free will caused that situation when it could have caused a different one. Such an entity can never lose or gain dignity, because it simply does not exist.

In the face of an insult, we will try to ensure that our image, which is very valuable for life in society, is not damaged; that the error is repaired as much as possible, etc. But an insult should never make us feel that we have lost our dignity. How could something someone says make us no longer "worthy"?

And as for the fear of making a fool of ourselves, the more we see everything that happens as natural phenomena, the more likely it is that we feel much less discomfort at something that is considered ridiculous, and the more likely we will even be able to laugh at what has happened to us.

# 24

# ENVY

According to the Oxford English Dictionary, envy is "the feeling of mortification and ill-will occasioned by the contemplation of superior advantages possessed by another."

We do not feel this whenever someone has something that we do not; if that were the case, we would be constantly feeling envy. It depends on something unique about some people in particular. In order to feel sad or angry just because a person enjoys something, that person must be someone we hate, or at least feel some aversion towards. For the well-being of others to cause us envy, we must also believe that those who enjoy it do not deserve it, but we do. It does not occur to me how these feelings could arise without the belief in a self and some form of merit that, in one way or another, is given by the good or bad deeds committed by the self with its free will.

Envy and all the negative feelings we are discussing have played a role in our evolution. In this case, envy can be a strong stimulus for individuals to strive to obtain things that others possess. But, again, assuming the nonexistence of the self and free will has very positive consequences: the fact that someone enjoys something that we lack continues to be a stimulus, but sadness, anger, ill-will and mortification will probably not be a part of it. These consequences are often not apparent at first glance, which is why it is important to know and share them so that this topic is given the importance it deserves.

## 25

# DUTY

According to the Royal Academy of Spanish Language, duty is "what one has the obligation to do."

But do not panic! No one is going to try to do away with the concept of duty in social, family and business affairs. All these duties are rules that we have to comply with if we want to live in society; they are the rules that have been established for life in community and no one wants to eliminate them.

I refer to a more abstract concept of duty, one which we have when we ask ourselves if we are doing "what *we have to do* in life." Sometimes we have the feeling that we should do something like having children, looking for a stable partner, or getting a better-paying job, because it is something that "must be done." Wondering what we should do, as if there is something that should be *chosen* to do, is a bit like wondering about the meaning of life. If life has no meaning, there is essentially nothing we should do either.

Once we have reflected and taken action, wondering if that is really what we should be doing does not make any sense.

When you have several options to choose from, what you choose will always be the result of how the phenomena related to that topic occur in your brain. Aside from the obvious considerations of not harming anyone with your actions and other social norms, there is no such thing as "what you should do." If you feel like spending an afternoon lying in a hammock, you might think that you should be working instead, earning money, or something else. Not because you need to, but because "it is not okay to be lazy." That is the kind of duty that does not make sense. If we stop and think about it, there are many things that we do or stop doing just because we are told that "they should be done" or that "they are not right," albeit in a very subtle way.

Of course, it is very healthy for our nature to lead us to reflect on what seems important to us and to do everything possible so that everything goes as we wish. But, once this is done, continuing to ask ourselves if we are as good parents, children, husbands, or friends as we should be is like asking ourselves if a tree should be taller or bear more fruit.

# 26

# REPENTANCE AND REMORSE

According to the Royal Academy of Spanish Language, to repent is "to feel regret for having done or not having done something" and remorse is "restlessness, internal regret that remains after doing what is considered a bad action."

Of course, realizing what the consequences of our actions are is a very healthy and convenient thing. And these feelings of regret drive us to take steps to repair the damage as much as possible, avoid similar future situations, etc. But a very common mistake is to think that we could have done something else, and that this depended on something that was not a previous circumstance, condition, or event, in our brain or somewhere else, but on our free will.

We have to understand that unfortunate actions happened, that the circumstances that led us to them were not under anyone's control and that in those circumstances we could not have done anything differently. Our will was the result of natural processes that occurred in our brain and there was no one in charge to direct anything. Once the measures have been taken to repair the damage as much as possible and to try not to repeat similar situations, the persistence of that restlessness and regret makes no sense; and remorse can lead to resentment, a grudge against oneself, which can become very destructive.

When our reaction is to think, "I am an idiot. How can I be such an idiot as to have done that? I do not deserve the well-being I have," we are blaming the self that with its free will could and should have done otherwise, and we are feeding negative feelings to ourselves based on the belief in something nonexistent.

When our reaction is to think, "Ugh, that action was a terrible mistake and what unpleasant consequences it had," and those thoughts give rise to a desire to examine the causes, repair the damage and take measures to try to prevent something like that from happening again, we are having a healthy reaction to what happened.

As we see, understanding the nonexistence of the self and free will makes our reactions more in line with reality and more appropriate for our well-being and that of the people with whom we live. The alleged negative effects of talking about the nonexistence of the self and free will are nothing more than misconceptions that take place when there is no understanding of this subject. There is nothing that changes for the worse when we understand what we are talking about. And there is no conflict that cannot be resolved by the fact of knowing that there is no free will, nor the self that allegedly has it.

# 27

# WILLPOWER

The psychologists of the Therapeutic Institute of Madrid wrote a thread in *Twitter* (now *X*), "When we talk about 'willpower' we usually refer to a kind of motivation that emanates from the individual alone, as if it were intrinsic, as if it were born from him without greater external influence." "No one has more willpower than another; it is an empty construct that explains nothing."

We think of willpower as something akin to muscular endurance. We believe that being able to persist in an action depends on what we call willpower, but in reality, it simply depends on whether we want to do it or not. What is not so simple is to understand the large number of factors that influence a decision. If we consider going to the gym three days a week and we do not accomplish that, it is because the very complex phenomena that occur in our brain lead us not to really want it. The motives that drive us to do so are not as influential on us as we would like to think. We are probably more seduced by the idea of staying on the couch now than improving our health in the long run.

When someone persists in doing something, it is because they believe that they will feel better. As long as they believe that, there is no way they are going to quit. But if at any time their belief changes there will be no way for them to continue to do so. The "power" of the will is another of the incoherent attributes associated with an organism. If a person who supposedly has "low willpower" one day begins to persist in something, it is not because suddenly his "willpower" has increased a lot, but because he is now convinced that this is the option that will bring him the most well-being.

The following anecdote can shed a lot of light on this issue. There is a famous method with which many people have achieved to quit smoking in a single six-hour session of intense work. My friend Clemente García Novella, who has helped me a lot with this book, worked a few years with this method obtaining incredible results: in all that time, 70% of the people who tried to quit smoking with the help of Clemente succeeded (percentage measured after a year). Obviously, those people did not start by lacking willpower and then suddenly achieved it afterwards. What happened was that the right information, far more complicated than it seems, was finally exposed and properly perceived in the brains of the now happily ex-smoking organisms. They went on to have the necessary motivation, understanding and approaches.

We always do what we think will make us feel better. This can happen in very complicated ways that can make us think that this is not the case. For example, if someone "sacrifices" himself by going to work as a volunteer in a place where he will suffer many hardships, it may seem obvious to us that he does something that causes him more discomfort than well-being. But, as soon as we look hard enough, we will discover that the satisfaction of doing that work outweighs the discomfort of all the inconveniences. This can be very complicated, but it does not make any sense for someone to do something that they think is going to make them worse off. Whether the person is wrong or not is irrelevant. What matters is what they believe.

It is quite evident that we attribute the supposed willpower to a self that can direct it wherever it wants. And when we think that someone is not using this driving force as they should, we also blame that self because they *could* do it—which is what free will is for—but "they just do not feel like it."

## 28

## CONTROL

If there is no free will, how come we are able to control ourselves?

As a matter of fact, what we call "control" is merely a practical way of referring to how a series of causes and conditions configure some phenomena.

The word "control" suggests an authorship, an agency. When we say that the pancreas controls the level of insulin in the blood, the idea that tends to appear in our brain is that the pancreas is the author of that action of controlling. But the reality is that the pancreas is not the author of any action, as neither the brain nor the organism as a whole are. Everything that happens in the universe is a series of phenomena that happen because of prior causes and conditions. And, in fact, there is never a "someone who controls something" in any case; in any event. What we call "natural laws" configure how all phenomena happen.

But, again, when those phenomena happen in our brain we usually give explanations based on the erroneous concepts of self and free will. For example, when we feel the desire to assault someone and we refrain, we say that we "maintained control over ourselves." But what actually happens is that, in addition to the desire to start a fight, we also feel a desire not to do so, and the latter is more decisive. Both desires are natural phenomena that occur due to a very complicated series of causes and circumstances, they have not been "created" or "controlled." And the final decision not to start the fight is also a phenomenon shaped by prior causes, conditions, etc.

Still, we need language to be practical. For example, we say that an organism controls its temperature. However, the reality is that several elements in the body are sensitive to changes in temperature. When the temperature increases or decreases beyond a certain point, specific chain reactions occur that result in the decrease or increase of the body's temperature. But we know that the body does not "decide" to initiate these processes. If we want to be precise, we cannot say that "it" controls its temperature, because "it" does not exist as an entity capable of doing something to begin with. Everything that happens in an organism are just events, the organism "does" nothing.

But the idea of a self that "does things" is a simplification that is practical for us. When we say, "Joan is eating," we are greatly simplifying a series of events: the lack of nutrients causes certain reactions, the perception of these reactions causes intentions in Joan's brain, etc. And to say that Joan "controls" the amount of food that enters his digestive system is technically imprecise, although very practical. What actually happens is that the amount of food that enters Joan's digestive system is configured by an immense and very complicated number of processes.

In the organism known as Joan, there is no driver, no self that controls anything. Millions of processes result in food entering the digestive system and being digested. And not a single one of these processes is created by the organism, the self, the will, or any other entity or concept we can imagine. It is just as imprecise to say that the body controls its temperature as it is to say that Joan eats bread. The strictly correct way to describe what is happening in both cases would be to say that phenomena take place that result in the temperature being maintained at certain levels or that the food enters the organism known as Joan.

But the habitual use of language leads us to think that, indeed, there is a self in Joan that "creates" and "controls" much of what he "does." We go back to the body-mind dualism (organism-self) every time we use everyday language. And we should not abandon everyday language. Just as we can continue to say that the sun rises, we can and should use language in a practical way and say, "Joan is eating," or "The storm is discharging a lot of water," or "He eventually took control of himself and did not start a fight."

Thus, we use the subject "I" and the verb "to do" to describe phenomena that happen somewhere in the organism that we are. And we say, "I do things." This is a necessary simplification in order to communicate. But we must be aware that this way of speaking does not accurately describe what actually happens. Here is an example:

If I say, "I am writing a text," everyone understands what I mean and this way of speaking is very practical. But let us see how accurate the statement is:

First of all, what is that "me"? I am an organism. My legs, my chest, my stomach... they are not writing. Thus not all that organism that I am is writing. My hands are doing the writing. But are my hands writing indeed? Well, the hands do not actually "do" anything; the movements of the hands are the result of a very complicated series of nerve impulses. So where do those nerve impulses come from? From the brain. Thus, is the brain writing? Well, ideas and thoughts take place in the brain, and then the intention to look for words, etc. Yet the whole of the brain is not involved in these events, only a small part. Moreover, we have already seen that the brain is an object, an organ in which things happen but which, like all objects, organs or systems, does not "do" anything.

Alright, we are growing impatient... Who is writing? This question does not have a strictly correct answer, because the grammatical subject does not correspond to a subject in reality. There is no such subject in reality. There is no me, no you, no she or he who does anything. Writing a text is a series of phenomena that are taking place. There is no agency, or authorship, in any event of all that occurs in the universe. It is impossible to describe exactly who that "someone" who does something is because there is no such someone. All that happens are events "configured by prior causes..." No one is behind the wheel. There is no steering wheel to begin with.

But do not panic. We are still alive because everything works according to those natural laws, and it seems that "everything is quite under control." The probability that we will stay alive and that everything will continue to work more or less "well" is very high. The probability that the sun will also "rise" tomorrow is very high.

# 29

# RESPONSIBILITY

When we say that someone is responsible for their actions, we are generally assuming that those actions were originated by the free will of a self, and that the person could have acted differently. But we have seen that neither that free will nor that self exist. And we know that nothing can happen differently than how it has been configured by the previous causes and conditions. Therefore, it is not coherent to speak of responsibility in that sense. The fact is that the organism we are talking about is where intentions and actions have been caused by natural phenomena. An organism is neither the cause nor the creator of the events that occur in it.

It is specifically in the brain of an organism where everything happens that will generate actions whose consequences can make us think of responsibility. But to believe that an object, a three-pound piece of gray matter, is actually responsible for what happens in it is just as absurd as to believe that the Earth is responsible for the earthquakes that occur on it.

The concept of responsibility becomes important when forming communities. The actions of a person on a desert island would simply have consequences; no conflict of responsibilities would arise. But for a society to function properly, its members must enjoy certain rights. And to secure these rights, we need to assign obligations. These include performing certain actions and not performing others. Therefore, when events occur in an organism that lead to actions that violate the rights of others, procedures need to be put in place to resolve the conflict in the best possible way. This is very complicated, and the idea that in a human organism there is a self, responsible for governing it with its free will, greatly simplifies the way of organizing societies and, especially, the measures to be taken in the face of conflict. These measures consist largely of punishing, causing suffering, or even killing the organism in which natural phenomena have occurred, in the absence of which the conflict would not have been triggered. The objective is to attack that self that governs the organism, to make it suffer or even kill it for having caused the conflict with its presumed free will.

But today we have the knowledge and tools to build a far more understanding, informed and effective society to achieve the greatest possible well-being for all its members. Today we know that an organism is the result of a very complex series of causes and circumstances that include millions of years of interrelated processes. But what that organism is not—or anything else in the universe—is the creator, the origin, the ultimate cause of any action or event. Therefore, we can use the term "responsible" in a practical way to refer to the organism where natural phenomena have occurred that led to certain consequences. With this understanding of what is actually happening, we will be able to attain the best possible state for the whole of society through the most effective measures, put in place to manage the positive or negative effects of those consequences. With this understanding, we can use the term "responsibility" in a much more realistic way; one that does not lead us to feel hatred or contempt.

If it is not possible to get rid of the term "responsibility" (and it does not seem to be), it should remain as a term that we use figuratively, just like we continue to say that the sun rises although we know that it does not "rise" because it is relatively still regarding the Earth. Similarly, we can continue to say that someone is responsible for something by referring to the relationship between the natural phenomena that occur in their brain and the consequences of those phenomena, although we know that the idea that an organism is responsible for something does not make any sense.

# 30
# GUILT

This word has several meanings. The Royal Academy of Spanish Language includes that of "the fact of being the cause of something." As an example, it says, "the rain was guilty of the ruined harvest."

Yet we understand that the rain is the result of a series of processes. We understand this use of *guilty* would mean "the fact of being the cause of something," as the fact of being part of the series of processes and elements that have led to the occurrence of that something.

There is an important difference between saying that the rain was guilty of the ruined harvest and saying that the clouds were guilty because they could have made the rain fall somewhere else. This would be a mistake because the composition of these clouds and all their characteristics played an important role in the development of events, but everything is the result of prior causes and conditions. Clouds have not created themselves; they have not caused themselves to be a certain way. They are as they are because of how the events that have made them so have occurred. And, of course, they cannot make the phenomena that occur in them develop differently—they could not have made the rain fall elsewhere.

This said, everything that happens in an organism, including thoughts, intentions and actions, are phenomena equally configured by previous causes and circumstances. As complicated as these phenomena are, it would be a mistake to think that an organism is guilty of something because it could have made its intentions and actions happen differently. The composition of that organism and all its characteristics played an important role in the development of events; but, again, all this is the result of prior causes and conditions. The organism has not created itself; it has not caused itself to be a certain way. It is as it is because of how the events that have made it so have occurred. And, of course, it cannot make the phenomena that take place in it develop differently than they do. A thought, an intention, or an action, are not something that an organism creates; it is the result of a very complex series of natural events that occur in it.

If we understand this, we will also understand the *guilt* of an organism in that sense of "being the cause of something," as the fact of being part of the series of processes and elements that have led to the occurrence of that something. If we understand that a person who performed a harmful action could not have acted otherwise and that all events are shaped by previous causes and conditions, our consideration of that person changes in very interesting ways, many of them already described in other chapters of this book.

These ideas often arouse the fear that a society could not be maintained, that chaos would reign, that we would not be able to take action against crime and many other nonsensical conclusions. These fears are totally unfounded, as we will see in the following chapters.

# 31

# JUSTICE

There are many definitions of justice. The simplest is "to give everyone their fair share." In the Spanish version of Wikipedia, we find a more thorough concept: "Justice is the set of guidelines and criteria that establishes a fitting framework for relationships between people.... This set of guidelines and criteria has a cultural foundation based on a broad consensus amongst individuals of society about right and wrong and other practical aspects of how relationships between people should be organized."

It is obvious that the more knowledge we have of ourselves and of the world of which we are a part, the better prepared we will be to administer justice. To give everyone "their fare share" we must learn everything we can about ourselves and everything that happens to us.

But sometimes, something that we had not taken into account changes the way we see the world and seems to complicate things. For example, when we say that a person could have never acted otherwise, we almost always make the mistake of assuming that, therefore, all actions are involuntary. This creates an enormous confusion about this issue. As we saw in the chapter dedicated to voluntary and involuntary actions, in the former "there are, as well as the perceptions and movements necessary to perform the action, other phenomena such as intention, reflection and deliberation. And that difference is extremely important, especially when considering the consequences and possible implications of those actions."

A voluntary action, carried out after consideration, gives us information about how thoughts and intentions tend to be structured in that organism. If a person assaults another after considering the possible consequences, we are faced with facts that make us foresee future dangerous events. That is why we act in a completely different way than we do when faced with an action that is the result of a spontaneous or reflex reaction.

When damage occurs as a result of a pattern of dangerous behaviors that could be repeated, we take steps to prevent future damage and repair the present damage as much as possible. The administration of justice, the "just treatment," sometimes will inevitably cause harm to some people, as in the case of fines and imprisonment. The better informed we are about how and why the events that affect us occur, the more we can reduce those damages to the necessary minimums and the more effective our measures will be. In this way, we will achieve the best possible result for the whole of society.

## 32

# PUNISHMENT AND REWARD

Punishment: "The infliction of a penalty or sanction in retribution for an offence or transgression."
Reward: "A recompense or return given to (or received by) a person for some service, merit, or favour, or for hardship endured."
(Oxford English Dictionary)

Curiously, people argue that punishment and reward have no meaning without the existence of free will, since they are precisely unbeatable examples of how the will is configured by prior causes and conditions, and is directed towards where these lead it. With these measures, it is possible to prevent someone from repeating harmful actions, dissuade other people from taking similar actions, encourage desirable behaviors, avoid spirals of violence, and a long etcetera. It is impossible to organize a society without using these resources. Therefore, there is no point in discussing whether knowing that there is no free will would allow us to continue punishing and rewarding certain behaviors or not.

Even so, it is argued that without free will we would not have a good reason to punish anyone. This is clearly false—we frequently apply punishments knowing that we could not have acted otherwise. With children we use punishment for educational purposes, to redirect and correct their behavior. And of course, we punish and reward our pets as well. This does not conflict either with the love we have for them or with the pursuit of their greatest possible well-being.

We can also see that, on many occasions, recognizing the nonexistence of free will does not prevent us from punishing the actions of adults. For example, people are severely fined when they do not stop at a red light. We do not care if that person has free will or not; if they had not seen the traffic light; if it turns out that they are a very distracted person and cannot pay enough attention, etc. If they do it several times, in addition to fining them again, their driving license will be revoked. And if they keep driving without a permit, they will probably end up in jail. We simply cannot allow people to act like this. We know there would be terrible consequences. And this is enough for us. We do not need to believe in free will to punish or reward an action.

What is absolutely necessary is to find the fairest way to apply these measures. For this, we must recognize that all actions are configured by natural phenomena, causes and conditions and not by nonexistent entities such as the self, with nonexistent capacities such as free will. We must be aware that a person who acted could not do otherwise. Given these considerations, we do not use punishment and reward with a moral criterion. We do not punish or reward someone to cause them suffering or pleasure as retribution for their actions, but to achieve the effects of those measures in shaping their future behavior and in the functioning of society.

Finally, we must carefully assess the damage and benefit caused by punishment and reward. This way we can achieve the desirable effects of these measures and avoid their use leading to negative intentions and consequences such as hatred, revenge, humiliation, deification, arrogance, and contempt.

# 33

# REVENGE

According to the Oxford English Dictionary, revenge is "hurting, harming, or otherwise obtaining satisfaction from someone in return for an injury or wrong suffered at his or her hands."

For our ancestors to survive, the desire to harm those who would have harmed them, or to kill those who would have killed one of their own, surely played a fundamental role. Probably in this way it was possible to maintain violence and hatred at tolerable levels for society. That desire is still strongly ingrained in us, but the way we are considering the causes of our behavior makes us see it differently. Although our instinctive reactions can change a lot, little or nothing, our most thoughtful decisions and conclusions will likely change a lot.

Although sometimes it seems that the idea of revenge has that sweet taste that is attributed to it, reflection leads us to the conclusion that harming someone just for the sake of giving us satisfaction is not a good way to resolve conflicts and does not give us the peace we want.

# 34

## FORGIVENESS

**Forgive:**
1. "To give up resentment against or pardon (an offender)." (Oxford English Dictionary)

2. "To grant relief from payment." (Merriam-Webster)

I do not think "giving up" or "granting relief" to anyone from anything makes much sense. A very common way of understanding forgiveness seems to convey that we are removing something, such as when we forgive someone for the money they owe us and leave the account at zero. It seems that from the moment in which we forgive something, we act as if whatever is forgiven never happened, or as if it has passed on to another category of matters—those that are forgiven.

What we need is to dialogue; understand what happened and analyze the causes and circumstances, both internal and external, which resulted in the action that caused the damage. Once we understand *why* something happened, once measures have been taken so that it does not happen again, and once the damage has been repaired as much as possible, etc., I think it makes much more sense to talk about conflict resolution than to forgive.

But we may not be able to fix the issue in such a satisfying manner. We may believe that the circumstances that led to these actions still remain and that, therefore, similar situations may occur again. Or maybe the mere presence of that person causes us great pain because the damage was very serious. For these and other reasons, we may not want to keep in touch with that person. Not because "we cannot forgive," but because it has not been possible for that rapport and other necessary circumstances to occur. But not reaching a rapport does not have to lead us to hold a grudge against anyone, as is usually thought to happen when something "is not forgiven." A grudge is like an echo of hate that extends over time, and we have already seen that hatred makes little sense in any scenario.

Whether or not we can resolve a conflict satisfactorily will depend on many factors, but the concept of forgiveness does not bring much to the table. It is a matter of understanding, communication, intentions, repair of damages and measures for the present and the future.

In the documentary *Human*, we see a beautiful example of the resolution of a serious conflict. A man convicted of killing his wife tells us that his mother-in-law visited him frequently in prison and, treating him very affectionately, helped him understand where his tendency to violence came from and to behave in a totally different way. I do not think his mother-in-law "forgave" him for killing her daughter. I do not think she "gave up" or "disregarded" anything, or "granted this man relief" from any debt, but she was tremendously sympathetic and knew how to communicate with her son-in-law, with a wonderful result, in one of the most difficult situations we can imagine.

# 35

# PERSONAL RELATIONSHIPS

In any type of relationship, it becomes apparent that our feelings are something that "happens" to us and not something we control. These feelings depend on a lot of factors. That is why, sometimes, we do not even get to understand the causes that enable a relationship to last for years or come to an end.

However, we tend to think that everything depends on a single variable—to love someone enough. "Love conquers all." This is a myth akin to willpower. We think that love is what makes a relationship valuable to those involved, that our feelings are the cause of something wonderful happening between us or what ends the relationship. We tend to explain our actions as the manifestation of something from within us. But it is not that we possess "things" like love or willpower that lead us to perform loving or persistent actions. We simply perform those actions.

"A lover has no love (and may all the Romeos in the world forgive me); he loves. A criminal does not possess aggressiveness; he is aggressive. And this grammatical shift that we commit from the verb (the action, the behavior) to the noun (the thing) corresponds precisely to the process of objectification, nouning, reification (taking the Latin root *res-rei)*, a process so common and usual that we are not even aware of how much we abuse it. And yet, reification constitutes another classic categorical error (confusing verbs with nouns) in the traditional explanation of behavior..." (These are the words of Esteve Freixa i Baqué, Professor of Epistemology and Behavioral Sciences, PhD in Psychology and Licentiate in Philosophy and Letters).

A relationship does not evolve in one way or another because we want it to. We think that everything depends on the existence of love and that such love will make things go well. But the process is rather the opposite—everything that happens between people shapes the feelings they have for one another. This may seem obvious when we stop to think about it, but sometimes our responses reveal that we are not so sure about it. For example, we often blame a person whose feelings have changed, as if we could make those feelings unfold differently.

When a certain conflict arises, a very common reaction is to try to find out who is to blame. Once we have a clear idea of who the culprit is, we burden them with the shame of having done something "wrong" when they could have done something else. And finally, we assign them all the work—they must solve that which created the conflict, since it is their problem. And it may actually be that the cause of the problem is within one of the people involved. But when we talk about guilt whilst believing that the person could have done something else in those same circumstances, we are building upon an erroneous foundation which will lead us to erroneous conclusions. That person could never have done anything else.

Faced with these types of ideas, the usual response is that nothing can be done in that case, that anything goes and things like that. A crass mistake. Understanding that behavior is shaped by causes and circumstances is precisely what makes it possible to take actions to contribute to future behavior being different from the past, in a way that is more beneficial to us. The better we comprehend all the processes that affect us in any aspect of our life, the more adequately the intentions and actions will be generated in our brains to reach the best possible situation.

Thus, conflicts can often be resolved and difficulties can be overcome, which is very important. And, in other cases, the best possible situation will be to end a relationship. This does not depend on whether we "love someone a lot or a little" or whether we have more or less willpower, but on what conclusions the evolution of the thoughts and feelings that arise in us leads us to.

In personal relationships, we are seeing more and more evidence that the aforementioned self does not exist; the self that governs the organism and decides, for example, to love a person. We must continue to use grammatical pronouns, such as "I" and "we," for practical reasons; but we must not lose sight of the reality that the type of "I" we are talking about (the self) does not exist. When I say, "I do this," or "I love you," the fact I am referring to is that "these events occur in this organism."

Many people find these ideas unpleasant because they think they take something away from us. But if we have the feeling that we are "losing" something, it is because we believed in something that we now realize does not exist. Therefore, we have lost nothing. Rather, realizing this reality makes us more likely to direct our thoughts and actions towards a better outcome in all kinds of relationships and, in general, in all aspects of our lives. And no, it does not make us enjoy anything less as a result. I do not see how a greater understanding of what happens can make us lose anything. Understanding how our eyes, our nervous system and everything related to vision works does not make everything around us seem less beautiful. The same goes for everything we learn about ourselves and our environment. If anything, thanks to this understanding, everything that happens seems even more fascinating to us.

# V

# CONCLUSIONS

## 36

## CONCLUSIONS

When we are first confronted with ideas that we deem interesting, we hope that they will improve some aspects of our lives. But often this is not the case. Sometimes it even seems impossible that we could adapt to such a way of seeing things. However, if certain ideas are useful, they can change the lives of those who accept them. But for that to happen it takes much more than just reading a book.

In these cases, as in many others, we are used to expecting results very soon. What can bring real change to our lives is to keep reflecting upon it. And share those ideas. The old mental schemes and the usual way of reacting to what happens to us are not going to change soon. We need to keep these ideas in mind for a long time and in many different situations.

Once we have realized something, what makes our lives better is to be consistent with it. This seems easy to achieve, but on many occasions we feel that we cannot live according to our ideas. The fact is that changing our way of behaving based on what we keep learning makes our lives extraordinarily fulfilling, but we have to learn how to deal with its side effects: some of those changes will surprise and upset many people and we will be met with all kinds of reactions. This is an insurmountable obstacle for many people who even try to convince themselves that certain changes are not actually desirable. Thereby, the phrase "if you do not live as you think, you will end up thinking as you live" is fulfilled.

The fear of the consequences of living according to our ideas can cause us to continue behaving in the most conventional manner, as many people expect from us. In this way, we manage to avoid many conflicts. But we are actually undermining our happiness and heading towards a sad reality. On one hand, because these conflicts could lead to changes that would free us from elements that generate discomfort in our lives. On the other hand, we are condemning ourselves to ways of life that are probably not going to satisfy us.

The solution to this is not more willpower or courage. What we need is to delve deeper into what we have realized and all its consequences. Understanding a situation and its solution are often one and the same. There comes a time when these changes occur "by themselves" and we have the feeling of not doing anything, because our will is simply directed to acting in a way following our understanding. And the same goes for our feelings about what happens to us.

Taking time to reflect on the topics covered in this book can diminish reactions such as hatred, low self-esteem and many others without making us feel that we are doing anything about it. Therefore, although some of the things that happen to us continue to cause us some harm, our well-being will increase tremendously because we will avoid that large part of our suffering that was the consequence of unfounded beliefs.

Ultimately, we can find a lot of peace in realizing that we are nothing more and nothing less than part of that wonderful nature from which we felt in some way separated by the beliefs in a god and a soul, or a self with capacities such as free will. We can ask ourselves the big questions without any fear, we can find answers that help us understand the world of which we are part, and we can give meaning to our lives by sharing and caring for everything we deem valuable.

# WHERE TO FIND MORE INFORMATION

Virtually all of the books and videos I discuss are available only in English. Here I will cover only those that I consider to be most useful to start learning about these topics, in the order that I believe to be most appropriate for someone who has not read or heard much about free will and the self. Much more information can be accessed at **www.fascinaos.com** (be fascinated).

I suggest starting with Alex O'Connor, a philosopher and well-known British *YouTuber*. He talks about free will in several videos on his *YouTube* channel. I recommend seeing "Why Free Will Doesn't Exist" first.

Sam Harris is the philosopher and neuroscientist who has made the topic of free will and the self known to the general public. I recommend watching his lecture "The Delusion of Free Will" on *YouTube,* in which he practically sums up his best-seller book, *Free Will.* I also recommend reading this book, which is very brief and revealing.

Sabine Hossenfelder, a German physicist and science popularizer, has two very educational and fun videos on her

*YouTube* channel: "You don't have free will, but don't worry" and "I don't believe in free will. This is why."

Esteve Freixa i Baqué, Professor of Epistemology and Behavioral Sciences, PhD in Psychology and Licentiate in Philosophy and Letters, is an authority in the study of behavior. I recommend the video of the interview he granted us on the *YouTube* channel *Razón o fe* (Reason or faith). The video is called *"El libre albedrío y el yo: 5. ¿Qué dice la ciencia?* (Free will and the self | 5 | What does science have to say?)" I also recommend the video *"El libre albedrío no existe* (Free will does not exist) - Esteve Freixa i Baqué" on the *enGramaPsico YouTube* channel.

Jerry Coyne, an American biologist, has a couple of video lectures in which he perfectly explains the nonexistence of free will and the beneficial effects for society as a result of understanding these issues. I recommend watching both lectures because there is very valuable and different content in both: "INR5: Jerry Coyne 'You Don't Have Free Will'" and "Jerry Coyne: Free will Zagreb."

Alex O'Connor exposes the inconsistency of compatibilism in another of his videos: "Compatibilism Debunked | Free Will and Determinism."

Robert Sapolsky, an eminent professor of biology and neurology, published his book *Determined. A science of life without free will*, in 2023. In this book, which I strongly recommend, we find an exhaustive review of the main arguments in favor of the existence of free will, which it masterfully refutes, and an extensive and magnificent explanation of scientific knowledge crucial for understanding this subject. As Sapolsky says in the book, if we consider the results obtained in the study of all relevant scientific disciplines, there is no place for free will. Among the numerous videos of his interviews on *YouTube*, I recommend starting with "Robert Sapolsky: Justice and morality in the absence of free will | Full [Vert Dider] 2020."

Gregg Caruso, philosopher and director of the Justice Without Retribution Network, includes on his website **greggcaruso.com** links to his books and lectures on how to improve many aspects of society. There are also several videos of his on *YouTube* among which I recommend "The dark side of free will | Gregg Caruso | TEDxChemungRiver."

At minute 3:25 of the video "Daniel Dennett - What is free will?" on the *YouTube* channel *Closer To Truth* (the 6-minute one, there are two videos with that name), Dennett defines free will as "our capacity to see probable futures, futures that seem like they are going to happen, in time to take steps so that something else happens instead." I recommend watching this and other videos of Dennett to understand the viewpoint of who probably is the best-known compatibilist at present.

Uri Maoz, professor of computational neuroscience, is the director of the Neurophilosophy of Free Will Project, endowed with seven million dollars, five of which come from the Templeton Foundation (whose intention in also financing another multi-million dollar project on the same subject was to "improve our understanding of free will in science, philosophy and theology"). In his short video "Is free will an illusion? | Uri Maoz | Big Think," we can witness a puzzling final statement, "Do I have free will depends, of course, on the definition. In the sense that the world could go one way or another way depending on my decision, no, I don't think I have that power. But to the extent that I can act according to my desires and my wishes, yes, I think I can. I wish to be here and here I am."

Jerry Coyne, in his article *Dan Dennett: misguided about free will, accurate about Templeton,* proves the incoherence of compatibilism and how—with its redefinitions and multiple interpretations—it resembles sophisticated modern theology. It also unmasks the Templeton Foundation's attempts to reconcile theology with science.

In another of his articles, *Templeton 'dialogue' about free will (hint: they're for it),* Coyne shows us how Templeton's multimillion-dollar projects are heavily influenced by their desire for science to show that free will *does* exist.

Lawrence Krauss, at minute 30:48 of his interview with Sapolsky, "The Illusion of Free Will," explains why he finds it liberating and energizing to recognize that there is no cosmic meaning to the universe and that there is no free will.

Learn more at **www.fascinaos.com** (be fascinated).

# QUOTES ABOUT FREE WILL

**Albert Einstein:** "I do not believe in free will. Schopenhauer's words: 'Man can do what he wants, but he cannot will what he wills,' accompany me in all situations throughout my life and reconcile me with the actions of others, even if they are rather painful to me. This awareness of the lack of free will keeps me from taking myself and my fellow men too seriously as acting and deciding individuals, and from losing my temper."

"Honestly, I cannot understand what people mean when they talk about the freedom of the human will. I have a feeling, for instance, that I will do something or other; but what relation this has with freedom I cannot understand at all. I feel that I will to light my pipe and I do it; but how can I connect this up with the idea of freedom? What is behind the act of willing to light the pipe? Another act of 'willing'? Schopenhauer once said: '*Der Mensch kann was er will; er kann aber nicht wollen was er will* (Man can do what he will but he cannot will what he wills).'"

**Yuval Noah Harari:** "Though 'free will' was always a myth, in previous centuries it was a helpful one. It emboldened people who had to fight against the Inquisition, the divine right of kings, the KGB and the KKK. The myth also carried few costs. In 1776 or 1945 there was relatively little harm in believing that your feelings and choices were the product of some 'free will' rather than the result of biochemistry and neurology.

But now the belief in 'free will' suddenly becomes dangerous. If governments and corporations succeed in hacking the human animal, the easiest people to manipulate will be those who believe in free will."

"People sometimes imagine that if we renounce our belief in 'free will,' we will become completely apathetic, and just curl up in some corner and starve to death. In fact, renouncing this illusion can have two opposite effects: first, it can create a far stronger link with the rest of the world, and make you more attentive to your environment and to the needs and wishes of others.... Second, renouncing the myth of free will can kindle a profound curiosity. If you strongly identify with the thoughts and desires that emerge in your mind, you don't need to make much effort to get to know yourself. You think you already know exactly who you are. But once you realize, 'Hi, this isn't me. This is just some changing biochemical phenomenon!' then you also realize you have no idea who – or what – you in fact are. This can be the beginning of the most exciting journey of discovery any human can undertake."

"Theologians developed the idea of 'free will' to explain why God is right to punish sinners for their bad choices and reward saints for their good choices.... This myth has little to do with what science now teaches us about Homo sapiens and other animals. Humans certainly have a will – but it isn't free."

**Charles Darwin:** "One doubts the existence of free will [because of] every action determined by heredity, constitution, example of others or teaching of others. This view should teach one profound humility; one deserves no credit for anything... nor ought one to blame others."

**Francis Crick** (Nobel Prize for the discovery of DNA structure): "You, your joys and your sorrows, your memories and your ambitions, your sense of personal identity and free will, are in fact no more than the behavior of a vast assembly of nerve cells and their associated molecules."

**Voltaire:** "A free will is an expression absolutely void of sense, and what the scholastics have called will of indifference, that is to say willing without cause, is a chimera unworthy of being combated."

**Mark Twain:** "Where there are two desires in a man's heart he has no choice between the two but must obey the strongest, there being no such thing as free will in the composition of any human being that ever lived."

**Baruch Spinoza:** "The mind is determined to this or that choice by a cause which is also determined by another cause, and this again by another, and so on ad infinitum. This doctrine teaches us to hate no one, to despise no one, to mock no one, to be angry with no one, and to envy no one."

**Lawrence Krauss:** "It's liberating and energizing to know both things (there is no free will and there is no cosmic meaning to the universe) because it makes you understand your place and it makes every moment more precious."

Printed in Great Britain
by Amazon